W9-BIN-722

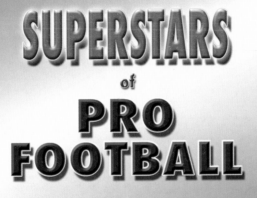

SUPERSTARS

of

PRO FOOTBALL

ADRIAN PETERSON

Stephen Currie

Mason Crest Publishers

Adrian Peterson

16146

Produced by OTTN Publishing in association with
21st Century Publishing and Communications, Inc.

Copyright © 2009 by Mason Crest Publishers. All rights reserved. No part of this
publication may be reproduced or transmitted in any form or by any means,
electronic or mechanical, including photocopying, recording, taping, or any
information storage and retrieval system, without permission from the publisher.

MASON CREST PUBLISHERS INC.
370 Reed Road
Broomall, Pennsylvania 19008
(866) MCP-BOOK (toll free)
www.masoncrest.com

Printed in the United States of America.

First Printing

9 8 7 6 5 4 3 2 1

Library of Congress Cataloging-in-Publication Data

Currie, Stephen, 1960–
  Adrian Peterson / Stephen Currie.
    p. cm. — (Superstars of pro football)
  Includes bibliographical references.
ISBN 978-1-4222-0548-8 (hardcover) — ISBN 978-1-4222-0832-8 (pbk.)
  1. Peterson, Adrian. 2. Football players—United States—Biography—Juvenile
literature. 3. Running backs (Football)—United States—Biography—Juvenile
literature. I. Title.
GV939.P477C87 2008
796.33092—dc22
[B]   2008025387

Publisher's note:
All quotations in this book come from original sources, and contain the spelling
and grammatical inconsistencies of the original text.

◄◄ CROSS-CURRENTS ►►

In the ebb and flow of the currents of life we are each influenced
by many people, places, and events that we directly experience or
have learned about. Throughout the chapters of this book you will
come across **CROSS-CURRENTS** reference bubbles. These bubbles
direct you to a **CROSS-CURRENTS** section in the back of the
book that contains fascinating and informative sidebars
and related pictures. Go on. ►►

«CONTENTS»

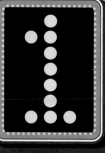

M! V! P!

Adrian Peterson grasped the football and sped toward the side of the field. A space had just opened up between two defenders, and he meant to plow right through it. As he barreled forward, the defenders dived for him. But all they caught was empty air. Adrian had already zoomed by.

About 15 yards from the **end zone**, Adrian paused. He changed direction and dashed for the opposing team's goal line. Speeding up again, he twisted past yet another defender. He had 10 yards to go . . . five yards . . . two . . .

No one could catch him. Adrian darted across the goal line and into the end zone. Touchdown! He tossed the ball from one hand to the other and waved to the crowd. Then he headed back to the field to celebrate with his teammates.

Adrian Peterson runs with the ball during the 2008 NFL Pro Bowl at Aloha Stadium in Hawaii. Adrian led all players with 129 yards rushing and was named the all-star game's Most Valuable Player.

Score!

This dramatic touchdown run took place during the second half of the 2008 **Pro Bowl**, the annual all-star game for players in the National Football League (NFL). The 2008 Pro Bowl was held in Honolulu, Hawaii. It pitted the stars of the NFL's National **Conference**, or NFC, against the top players from the American Conference (AFC). During the **regular season**, Adrian played for the Minnesota Vikings of the NFC, so he was on the NFC squad.

The game started poorly for Adrian and his teammates. At one point in the first half, the AFC

CROSS-CURRENTS

To learn more about the way in which the National Football League is organized, read "Conferences and Divisions." Go to page 46.

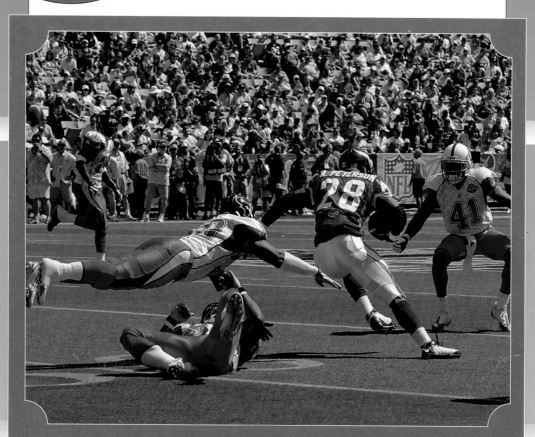

Adrian (number 28) splits defenders during a long run in the 2008 Pro Bowl. His two touchdowns in the game helped the NFC team defeat the AFC, 42 to 30.

led by 17 points. But the NFC's offense roared back. The team scored one touchdown. Soon after that, it scored another. Then Adrian completed his run down the sideline. Suddenly the game was tied. Moments later Nick Folk of the Dallas Cowboys kicked the **extra point**. Adrian's speed had helped put the NFC ahead for the first time in the game.

Adrian wasn't through, however. Late in the game the NFC reached the AFC's six-yard line. The team's coaches called for Adrian to carry the ball once more. Adrian dashed to his right, then cut back to the middle of the field. He sprinted through the defense and into the end zone for the second time that afternoon. Then he wrapped NFC teammate Shawn Andrews in a bear hug. A few minutes later the game was over. The NFC had come from behind to win, 42–30.

Two Goals

Players are paid extra to take part in the Pro Bowl, and many stars look forward to the game. Still, some of the NFL's top players choose not to play. Some feel they are too banged up after a long season. Others think they need a break from football for a while. Among the well-known players staying home in 2008 were Tom Brady of the New England Patriots and Antonio Gates of the San Diego Chargers.

Adrian never considered missing the game. To him, being picked for the Pro Bowl was a great honor. He was eager to show fans, coaches, and other players what he could do. Indeed, he came to Hawaii with two goals. The first was to help the NFC squad win the game. The other was to be chosen the game's **most valuable player**, or MVP—the player who does the most to help his team. As he said,

CROSS-CURRENTS

For more information about how the Pro Bowl differs from other all-star games, read "All-Star Games and the Pro Bowl." Go to page 47.

Go to page 47.

> **❝I'm dedicated to being the best, and that's what got me to this point. I came here with the mind-set of wanting to win the game.❞**

When the NFC completed its victory, Adrian reached the first part of his goal. The only question was whether he would also be named MVP. Adrian certainly had a strong case. Not only did he score those two touchdowns, he also ran with the ball for 129 yards. In the entire history of the Pro Bowl, only one player had ever **rushed** for more yards than that.

The Award

Adrian was not the only Pro Bowl star to excel. Rob Bironas of the AFC's Tennessee Titans kicked three field goals. Dallas Cowboys **quarterback** Tony Romo threw two touchdown passes, both to fellow Cowboy Terrell Owens. T. J. Houshmandzadeh of the

After being named MVP of the Pro Bowl, Adrian posed with the trophy. Adrian became just the second rookie to win this award. His 129 yards rushing was the second-highest total in the all-star game's history.

Cincinnati Bengals scored two touchdowns as well. Any of these men could have been named MVP—especially Terrell and Tony. Like Adrian, they had both played for the winning team.

In the end, the MVP voters chose Adrian. On this day, at least, he had been the best of the best. Adrian had met both his goals. He earned $40,000 for playing on the winning team—and received a brand-new Cadillac for being named MVP. Still, to Adrian, the MVP award was about much more than just a car. In his comments after the game, Adrian dedicated the award to Sean Taylor, a star player for the Washington Redskins who had been murdered earlier in the 2007 season.

Adrian's play at the Pro Bowl would have been impressive for anyone. It was especially remarkable, though, because Adrian was only 22 years old. He was one of the youngest players in the NFL, let alone at the Pro Bowl. Just one year earlier he had been playing football at the college level. For Adrian, the Pro Bowl had been a great ending to a fine season. Nevertheless, he believed he could improve in the future. As he told reporters,

"Can I top this? Yeah, you always set your bar high."

UPS AND DOWNS

Adrian Peterson was born on March 21, 1985, in Palestine, Texas. From early on he loved sports. That was no surprise; both his parents were athletes. Adrian's mother, Bonita Jackson, had starred on her college track team and participated in the Junior Olympics. Adrian's father, Nelson Peterson, played college basketball. And one of Adrian's uncles had played pro football.

As a small boy Adrian loved to be active. He once described his childhood in the small East Texas town this way:

"I ran around all the time. Never wanted to stop. Never wanted to sleep. I just kept going all day. . . .

From a young age, Adrian enjoyed being active and doing things outdoors. His family—and particularly, his father—encouraged Adrian's interest in sports and helped him to develop his athletic talents.

> When I started playing ball, my coaches said the same thing about how I played, that I could go all day. **"**

CROSS-CURRENTS

Read "Emmitt Smith" to find out more about the life and career of one of Adrian's favorite players. Go to page 48. ▶▶

His parents nicknamed him "All Day," or "AD" for short. The name has stuck with him ever since.

As Adrian got older he became interested in organized sports. He enjoyed track and basketball, but the sport he liked most was football. From the time he was seven, he played on local youth teams. Adrian also enjoyed playing pickup games with friends in the neighborhood. He also liked to watch games on television, especially if they involved his favorite NFL team, the Dallas Cowboys. His favorite Cowboy, Emmitt Smith, was a star **running back**. As a running back, Emmitt's main job was to carry the ball down the field toward the end zone. Adrian dreamed of playing for the Cowboys himself someday.

Hard Times

Growing up, Adrian was very close to his family. His father helped coach his football teams. His mother, a former track star, taught him about running. But when Adrian was just seven, his family suffered a terrible tragedy. Adrian's brother, Brian, was riding his bicycle one day when a drunk driver smashed into him. Adrian was playing football nearby and watched in horror as his brother tumbled to the ground. The accident ended Brian's life. He was only nine years old.

In 1998, when Adrian was 12, he got some more bad news: His father had been arrested. The federal government said that Nelson Peterson was part of a gang that sold crack cocaine. Nelson was put on trial and found guilty. He spent the next eight years in prison. Nelson's crime had a huge impact on Adrian. As he described it later:

"It was a hard time for me with my dad out of my life at a young age like that. At first it was real difficult. I just had to find a way to cope with it. We [had done] a lot of stuff together.**"**

Like many young people growing up in Texas during the 1990s, Adrian idolized Emmitt Smith, the star running back for the Dallas Cowboys. Smith ended his career with more rushing yards (18,355) than any back in NFL history.

Still, Adrian and his father kept in touch. They talked on the phone, and Nelson made sure to warn his son away from gangs and drugs. They also talked about football. Some of their discussions were about the Cowboys. But others were about Adrian's own football teams. Although Nelson couldn't see his son's games in person, he loved to hear Adrian talk about them over the phone.

High School

Adrian's games were worth talking about. Each year it became more and more obvious that Adrian was a gifted athlete. By the middle of

A crowd at Oklahoma Stadium watches the band perform before a football game. Adrian decided to attend the University of Oklahoma because the school's football program was considered one of the best in the country.

high school, he was one of the best players in Texas—and perhaps beyond. Like his hero, Emmitt Smith, Adrian mostly played running back. He was fast and strong, and he played hard. In 2002, his junior year, Adrian scored 22 touchdowns for the Palestine High School football team. That same season he rushed for over 2,000 yards. Both were outstanding totals.

CROSS-CURRENTS

To learn how colleges build their football programs by bringing in top high school players, check out "College Recruiting." Go to page 49. ▶▶

Word of Adrian's talents spread. **Scouts** from college teams began coming to watch him play. They hoped to convince Adrian to come to their schools to play football. The University of Arkansas was interested in Adrian. Texas A&M University was, too. So were the University of Miami, the University of Oklahoma, and many more. All of these schools offered Adrian the chance to get a college degree. They also offered him a way to reach the NFL. The NFL gets its players from college teams. Anyone who wants to play in the NFL has to play in college first.

In 2003 Adrian began his senior year of high school. It was his last high school football season—and it was also his best. He rushed for 2,960 yards and scored an amazing 32 touchdowns. Many football experts named him the best high school player in the nation. At the end of the season, Adrian took part in a high school all-star game that included students from all around the United States. He had never faced so many good players before. But Adrian did just fine. He scored two touchdowns in the game and gained 95 yards rushing. It was a fitting end to a great high school career.

Soon after the game Adrian announced that he had made up his mind about college. He would be going to the University of Oklahoma, which was not far north of his home in Palestine. Adrian had worked hard to get this far. As his mother said:

❝Adrian's a pretty unique kid. He's had big obstacles to overcome in his life. But with a lot of prayers, we made it from Point A to Point B.❞

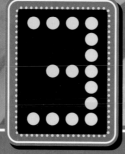

COLLEGE STANDOUT

Adrian was joining a strong college football program with a long history of success. Between 1945 and 2008 Oklahoma's football team, known as the Sooners, have won more games than any other college team. The Sooners have also captured more than 40 conference championships. And they have won seven national titles as well!

Adrian was also joining a team with a tremendous offense. The 2003 Sooners had scored the most points in team history. They had won one game 65–13 and another 77–0. Their quarterback, Jason White, had won the Heisman Trophy—an award given each year to the best college football player in the country.

The University of Oklahoma Sooners trot onto the field before the start of a game. In 2004, Adrian's first season on the team, Oklahoma was expected to compete for a national title.

Adrian hoped to be an important part of the powerful Sooner offense during his first year.

A Strong Beginning

That was not going to be easy. College freshmen usually lack the size and experience needed to compete with older players. It can also take time for new players to adjust to college life and to learn the team's plays. As a result very few freshmen star on their college teams. Many don't play at all.

Then again, Adrian was not an ordinary freshman. In high school, after all, he had been one of the best running backs in the country. He was big, strong, and fast. Oklahoma coaches expected that Adrian would play—and play a lot.

CROSS-CURRENTS

Read "The Heisman Trophy" to learn about the history of the major award given to college football stars. Go to page 50.

MOST VOLUBLE PLAYER
Gary Sheffield Speaks His Mind

SI's 2004
BASEBALL
AWARDS
by TOM VERDUCCI
Roger Clemens: Another Cy Young

Sports Illustrated

SPECIAL REPORT
>> NFL <<
INJURIES
WHY ARE
THERE SO MANY
SO SOON?

CHARLIE GARNER, BUCS

Freshman
Adrian Peterson
(Texas-born)
is Oklahoma's
newest weapon

SATURDAY SHOWDOWN
Oklahoma
vs. Texas

THE OTHER BIG ONE
USC vs. Cal

Adrian was pictured on the cover of *Sports Illustrated* before second-ranked Oklahoma's game against traditional rival Texas. In the game, Adrian ran for 225 yards as the Sooners defeated the fifth-ranked Longhorns, 12-0.

In early September the Sooners opened the 2004 season by defeating the Bowling Green Falcons. The Oklahoma offense scored 40 points in the victory. Football teams can move the ball forward by passing it or running with it, and the Sooners did both in this game. When they ran, they usually gave the ball to a player named Kejuan Jones. Jones had been on the 2003 Oklahoma team, and he had an outstanding game. He carried the ball 32 times and rushed for a total of 147 yards.

But Adrian saw playing time against the Falcons as well. He got the ball 16 times and scored a touchdown. Rushing for 100 yards is considered excellent for any running back; Adrian ran for 105 against Bowling Green in his first college game ever! Although he fumbled the ball twice, he managed to recover it each time. All in all it was a remarkable college debut for a freshman.

A Great Season

Adrian's second game was even better. Against the University of Houston, he rushed for 130 yards and scored two touchdowns. The Sooners relied on him more often in this game, too. Adrian had 25 carries, one more than all the other Sooners combined. The next week, Adrian scored two more touchdowns and ran for 183 yards. Though he was just 19, Adrian was becoming a star on one of the best college teams in the country.

The Sooners were a dominant team in 2004, and Adrian's running was a big reason for their success. On October 9, Adrian ran for 225 yards against Texas. Three weeks later he picked up 249 more against rival Oklahoma State. On November 20, he rushed for 240 yards and scored three touchdowns at Baylor. Finally, on December 4, Adrian scored three touchdowns once again as Oklahoma crushed Colorado in the conference championship game.

Adrian's only real disappointment came in the last game of the season: the Orange Bowl, held in Miami, against the University of Southern California. The winner of this game would be considered the national college champion. Adrian gained just 82 yards against a strong defense, and the Sooners lost badly. Still, it had been a great year for Adrian. Only two teams had held him below 100 yards. He had scored 15 touchdowns. He had carried the ball more often than any other college player. And his 1,925 rushing yards set a new record for a college freshman—and a new team record as well.

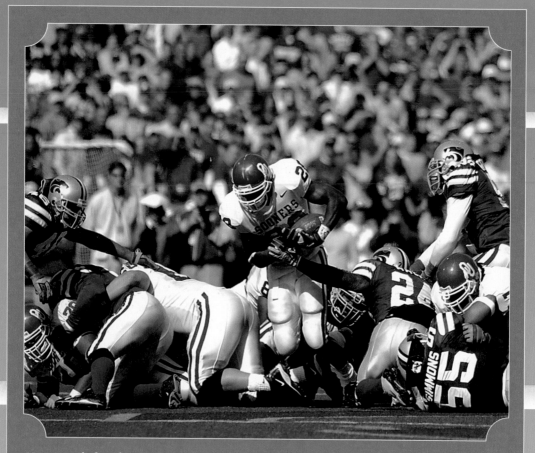

Kansas defenders try to slow Adrian down as he bursts through the line during a 2004 game. Few defenses were able to stop the powerful running back that season. Adrian ran for 130 yards against Kansas, and 1,925 yards overall.

These achievements earned Adrian plenty of attention. A group of experts named him a first-team All-American. Adrian even finished second in the voting for the Heisman Trophy. No freshman had ever come so close to winning the award.

Aches and Pains

Adrian began his second college season hoping to build on his strong freshman year. However, he got off to a slow start in Oklahoma's first game. During the entire first half, Adrian managed to gain just five yards.

He did better at the beginning of the second half, running for 43 yards during a series of plays and scoring his first touchdown of the year. But shortly after that, Adrian hurt his right ankle. He missed most of the rest of the game and ended the day with only 63 yards—the second-lowest total of his college career.

Luckily Adrian's ankle healed quickly. Not only did he return to the field the following week, but he played brilliantly. He rushed for 220 yards against the University of Tulsa and also caught two passes. In the next few weeks, he had other outstanding games, too. Against Oklahoma State, for instance, he averaged almost 10 yards per carry and picked up 237 total yards. Adrian also scored eight touchdowns in a four-game stretch. He finished the year with 14 touchdowns in all—just one short of his 2004 mark.

But in other ways, 2005 was frustrating for Adrian. The Sooners lost four games and did not contend for the national title. Adrian also had further problems with the ankle he had injured in the season opener. On October 1, he sprained the ankle during a victory over Kansas State and had to leave the game early. The injury kept him on the bench through most of the next two games, as well, and he missed the game after that altogether.

Adrian finally came back for good on October 29 against Nebraska. Fully healed at last, he ran 36 yards for a touchdown the first time he touched the ball. That was the story of Adrian's second year. When he was healthy, he was sensational. But the ankle injury kept him from matching his impressive numbers from 2004.

More Problems

Adrian seemed perfectly healthy as the 2006 season began. This time he got off to a great start. In each of the Sooners' first five games, he gained at least 100 yards rushing and scored at least one touchdown. On September 16 at Oregon, Adrian ran for 211 yards. A week later he scored three touchdowns in a 59–0 win over Middle Tennessee.

On October 14, the Sooners were scheduled to play Iowa State. Adrian was especially excited about this game. His father's prison term had ended at last, and Nelson Peterson was going to see his son play in person for the first time in years. Adrian described to a reporter how he felt about his father:

" Even though he was away so long, he was with me in spirit. He taught me the fundamentals of the game when I was little. . . . But our relationship is about more than football. He's my father, and he never stopped being that. Even though he made mistakes, I love him and I am proud of how he's turning his life around. **"**

Adrian wasted no time showing his dad what he could do. He began the game with a 40-yard run and scored a touchdown two plays later. By the middle of the fourth quarter, it looked as if he would reach 200 yards in a game for the seventh time in his college career.

Then disaster struck. With just over six minutes to play, Adrian took the ball at midfield and dashed for the goal line. He avoided an Iowa State player at the last second and dived into the end zone for a touchdown. But he landed awkwardly on his shoulder. The impact broke his collarbone. Team officials announced that he would miss the last seven games of the year. Unless the Sooners were invited to a **bowl game**, Adrian's season would be over.

New Plans

Adrian's injury was frustrating, but it forced him to think about his future. As a standout running back, he had expected to join the NFL after playing four years for the Sooners. But now he began to consider leaving Oklahoma at the end of his third season and signing with an NFL team right away.

It wasn't that Adrian was unhappy in Oklahoma. On the contrary, he loved playing for the Sooners. Many Oklahoma fans considered Adrian their favorite player, and his coaches and team-mates admired him, too. They saw him as modest, down-to-earth, and focused on the team. As head coach Bob Stoops explained:

" [Adrian is] a guy that's popular in the locker room because of how he works and his attitude and how he wants to be one of them, rather than be on the front page of any newspaper. He's as indifferent to that of any young guy I've ever been around. **"**

Adrian outruns a defender during Oklahoma's 37-20 victory over the Washington Huskies on September 9, 2006. Adrian gained 165 yards in that game. In his first six games of the 2006 season, Adrian ran for 935 yards and 10 touchdowns.

Adrian Peterson told *Sports Illustrated* that he enjoyed college life and was not sure if he was ready to leave school early. In the end, however, Adrian decided to make himself eligible for the 2007 NFL draft.

Adrian's real concern was his health. He was known for his hard style of play. Where other running backs tried to avoid tackles, Adrian preferred to run straight through the defense. His aggressiveness had helped him succeed. But it had also led to two major injuries in two years. If he got badly hurt in his senior season, it was possible that no NFL team would want him. His dream of reaching the pros would be gone forever. After much thought, Adrian decided to skip his final year at Oklahoma.

While Adrian was hurt, the Sooners won their conference championship yet again. That put them into the Fiesta Bowl against undefeated Boise State. Although Adrian's collarbone was much better, it was not completely healed. Some people advised him to skip the game. But Adrian insisted on playing. He played well, too, scoring two touchdowns. Most important, he made it through the game without injury. His desire to help his team impressed many observers. As one NFL scout put it:

❝That describes everything to me in terms of his [character]. Knowing he's a sure top 10 pick and with several people telling him not to risk it, he still comes back to play in the bowl game.❞

Adrian's college career had come to an end. His next step would be the NFL.

CROSS-CURRENTS

For details of Adrian's exciting final game with the Oklahoma Sooners, read "The 2007 Fiesta Bowl." Go to page 51. ▸▸

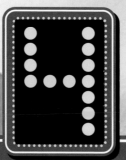

A TOP PICK

The NFL uses a **draft** to determine which pro teams college players can join. Teams take turns drafting, or selecting, players. The worst teams get the earliest picks; better teams must wait until later. A player is not required to join the team that picked him. But he may not sign a contract with any other team that year.

The draft is usually held in April. Long before the draft takes place, however, scouts from all 32 NFL teams already have plenty of information about the top players. These scouts have spent the previous fall watching college games in person and on TV. They have also talked to people who know the players well. All this research makes the scouts familiar with the best players, and they

In 2007, Adrian Peterson was expected to be one of the first players drafted. However, because of the injuries he had suffered in college, some teams were afraid Adrian could not stand up to the NFL's pounding defenses.

come to understand their strengths and weaknesses. The scouts then write reports on the players to help their teams decide which athletes to choose in the draft.

The Scouting Combine

Although scouts can get plenty of information by watching college football games, it can be tricky to compare players just by seeing them play. If a quarterback has a great game, it could be because he's a great quarterback—or it could be because the other team is not very good. Or suppose a running back rushes for only a few yards in a game. Is that his fault, or is it the fault of his teammates on the offensive line, who are supposed to keep the tacklers away from him? Players on good college teams often seem better than they really are, while players on bad teams may not have as many opportunities to show their true talent.

To help scouts compare players, the NFL invites the best prospects to Indianapolis, Indiana, each winter. There they take part in an event known as the **scouting combine**. The scouting combine is attended by scouts and other officials from all 32 teams. It has been described as a big job interview for football players. Team officials talk to the players they are most interested in drafting. They get reports on the players' health. They also find out how much weight a prospect can lift, how fast he can run, and how high he can jump. All this information helps the teams make their decisions.

CROSS-CURRENTS

Check out "The Scouting Combine" to find out more about this annual camp for prospective NFL players. Go to page 52. ▶▶

More Bad News

In 2007 Adrian Peterson was one of the young players invited to the scouting combine. Adrian had two goals for the event. Like everyone else, he wanted to show the scouts how well he could play. But Adrian also knew that many of the scouts questioned his health. They wondered whether his collarbone was fully healed. Some were concerned about his ankle, too. No one wanted to use a draft pick on an athlete who might not be able to play. So Adrian needed to show the scouts that he was in great physical shape.

At the annual scouting combine run by the NFL teams, Adrian ran one of the fastest times in the 40-yard dash. This showed teams that he was fully recovered from his injuries and ready to play.

The night before the combine was to begin, however, Adrian got a phone call at his hotel room in Indianapolis. His stepbrother, Chris Parish, had been shot and killed in Texas. It was a terrible tragedy, and Adrian was deeply upset. He considered going home and not participating in the combine. Adrian's agent told him that the NFL teams would understand if he made that decision. Even if Adrian went home, the agent said, he would probably be a high draft pick anyway.

But as Adrian considered his choices, he remembered something that Chris had told him a few days before:

❝You're gonna show 'em! Represent for all of us in Palestine. I'll be watching.❞

Touched by these words, Adrian decided to stay. Despite his grief, he took part in all the activities at the combine. He did extremely well, too, running the 40-yard dash in an amazing 4.38 seconds. Best of all, Adrian was able to convince some of the scouts that his body was fully healed. Adrian had indeed showed 'em—just as his stepbrother had predicted.

Draft Day

The draft was scheduled for April 28. Adrian had always dreamed that he would be chosen by his favorite team, the Dallas Cowboys. Unfortunately the Cowboys had one of the later picks, and most experts thought Adrian would be chosen long before Dallas made its selection. Some writers believed that Adrian might be taken as high as third. The Cleveland Browns, who had that pick, had said they were interested in him. Others expected Adrian to go to the Arizona Cardinals, who picked fifth, or to the Minnesota Vikings, who had the seventh choice. Several experts thought that Adrian would be an especially good fit for the Vikings. As writer Peter Schrager put it,

❝Peterson's arguably the biggest playmaker in this entire draft, a relentless worker with Hall of Fame potential. . . . Peterson at 7 [that is, the seventh pick] could very well end up being the steal of the draft.❞

April 28 was a tense day for Adrian and his family. The stress grew as the first few teams to pick passed over Adrian and selected other players. The Browns picked an offensive tackle named Joe Thomas. The Cardinals passed over Adrian as well. But Adrian didn't panic—and soon enough his name was called. As many of the experts had predicted, Adrian was chosen by the Vikings as the seventh pick in the draft.

The Vikings were delighted to get Adrian. The team's coach, Brad Childress, had been deeply impressed with Adrian at the scouting combine. He liked Adrian's physical skills and his

CROSS-CURRENTS

If you are interested in learning about the history of Adrian's NFL team, read "The Minnesota Vikings." Go to page 52. ▶▶

Adrian smiles after being chosen by Minnesota in the NFL Draft, April 28, 2007. Although Adrian received a number-one jersey on draft day, when the 2007 season started Adrian was assigned number 28 for the Vikings.

full-speed-ahead approach to the game. He also approved of the way Adrian handled himself off the field. Brad described his interview with Adrian in Indianapolis this way:

> **"He was . . . big, bright-eyed. Sitting there and asking questions. You felt like you knew some things about him where you could just see crystal clear. The enthusiasm for the game gushed without him having to say much, where you could see the sparkle. Where you kind of know, this is real."**

A Dilemma

There was one problem with the Vikings drafting Adrian, however. Most NFL teams use one main running back, and Minnesota already had a good one. That was Chester Taylor, a five-year veteran who had joined the Vikings the season before. In his year with Minnesota,

Veteran Minnesota running back Chester Taylor (right) talks with Adrian during the team's 2007 training camp. Taylor had run for 1,216 yards and six touchdowns with the Vikings in 2006. He also caught 42 passes for 288 yards.

Chester had played well. He had rushed for more yards than most other running backs in the league. Team officials agreed that Chester had been one of the brightest spots on a mediocre team.

It was true that the Vikings had a particular need for good running backs. The team's quarterback, Tarvaris Jackson, was young and inexperienced. He had played just one season in the NFL. For that reason the Vikings' offense mostly relied on running the ball, instead of asking Jackson to throw lots of passes. That meant more chances for running backs to see playing time.

Still, it wasn't possible for both Chester and Adrian to play as much as they wanted. So Vikings officials decided that the two running backs would share playing time, at least at the beginning of the season. Some top draft picks might have complained about this decision, but Adrian did not. He said that he was fine with sharing the job, and he added that he looked forward to working with Taylor:

> **❝Whatever the team [needs]. If that is to have a running back tandem, then I'm all for that. . . . I think that will help me a lot playing with a guy like Chester. Just learning the ins and outs and some guidance. You know, you're never too good to . . . have advice from other guys.❞**

Training Camp

Before Adrian could play in any Vikings games, he had to sign a contract. As the seventh pick in the draft, he knew he would be paid plenty of money. In general the earlier a player is picked in the draft, the more money he makes. Adrian wanted a contract that would run for several years, too. Football players often have their careers shortened by injury, so Adrian wanted the Vikings to guarantee most of the money—that is, promise to pay him much of his salary even if he was too badly hurt to play.

Working out the details of the contract took time. But in July 2007, soon after **training camp** opened, the two sides reached an agreement. The Vikings offered Adrian a multiyear contract that guaranteed him $17 million no matter what. And if Adrian became a big star in the NFL, the contract could earn him as much as $40 million. Adrian signed quickly and headed off to training camp.

After signing a big contract with the Vikings, Adrian reported to the team's training camp. While there, he practiced hard to be ready for the 2007 season. In camp, coaches and teammates praised Adrian's talent and work ethic.

The Vikings' training camp was held in Mankato, Minnesota. Mankato is only about 75 miles from the Metrodome in Minneapolis, the stadium where the Vikings play their home games. At training camp Adrian worked hard to get himself into shape for the 2007 season. He also got to know his teammates and coaches. At the same time, he impressed the people around him with his skills and his attitude. As new teammate Tony Richardson said,

> **[H]e's a very intelligent young man. You just pretty much tell him what to do and how to go do it, and he goes out there and does it full speed. He has all the tools, is a very smart kid, and he'll fit into our [team] just fine.**

In August the Vikings played four **preseason** games. These games are not part of the regular football season and do not count in the standings. While teams hope to win preseason games, coaches mainly use them to get players used to game conditions. Adrian got plenty of playing time during the preseason. Mostly he played well. In fact, he was the Vikings' biggest star in the second game; he rushed for 70 yards and scored a touchdown in a victory over the New York Jets. Perhaps more important, Adrian showed no signs of being bothered by his old injuries. As the preseason schedule came to an end, Adrian was ready for the regular season to begin.

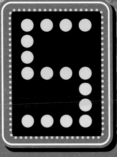

ROOKIE SENSATION

W hen the 2007 NFL regular season began, the Vikings opened with a home game against the Atlanta Falcons. Adrian Peterson was on the field to start the game. In fact he was the first Minnesota player to handle the ball; he caught the opening **kickoff** and returned it 22 yards.

The Vikings' coaches then turned to Chester Taylor. Chester carried the ball three times in the first few minutes of the game. Soon after that, though, he injured his hip and had to leave the game. Adrian quickly took his place—and made his presence known. On the Vikings' next possession, Adrian carried the ball four times for a total gain of 29 yards.

As it turned out, Adrian was only getting warmed up. In addition to his 22-yard kickoff return, he finished the game with 19 carries for 103 yards. He also caught a short pass and ran with it 60 yards for a touchdown. The Vikings won the game easily, and Adrian was a big part of the victory. It was a promising start to Adrian's pro career.

More Success

Adrian played well in the next few games, too. With Chester recovering from his injury, Adrian led the Vikings' offense. In the second

Adrian runs with the ball during a 2007 game. The rookie running back had an immediate impact, rushing for more than 100 yards in three of his first four games as a professional.

week of the season, he carried the ball 20 times and rushed for 66 yards. Both figures led his team. He also caught four passes for a total of 52 yards. A week later Adrian scored a touchdown, totaled 102 yards on 25 carries, and caught three more passes for another 48 yards.

Chester returned to the Vikings in the fourth week of the season, but Adrian continued to be a vital part of the Minnesota offense. He ran for 112 yards against the Green Bay Packers that week and returned a kickoff 51 yards as well. At that point Adrian had played in four professional games—and had rushed for 100 yards or more in three of them. That was an impressive statistic for any running back. It was especially outstanding for a player who had just joined the NFL.

Adrian's teammates already knew how good he was. Now players and coaches on other teams began to notice him, too. Joe Barry, a coach for the Detroit Lions, was especially impressed with Adrian's range of skills:

> **"He can run, he can catch, he can pass-block, he's tough. He's an inside runner, an outside runner. He's a guy who can get you the tough, short yards, and he's a guy who can break one for 70 [gain 70 yards on a single carry]."**

New Records

On October 14 the Vikings went to Chicago to play the Bears. That day, Adrian was almost unstoppable. He returned several kickoffs in the game, one of them for 53 yards. He scored three touchdowns as well, leading Minnesota to a 34–31 victory. Most remarkable of all, he rushed for 224 yards, double the total he had gotten against Green Bay the week before.

By rushing for 224 yards, Adrian set two new records. First, he shattered the Vikings' old single-game rushing record of 200 yards. Second, he set a record that involved the Bears. The Bears have a longer history than almost any other team in the NFL. Since joining the league, they have played over 1,200 games. Yet no opponent had ever rushed for that many yards against them. Adrian was the first.

It was an amazing game for Adrian. But there was more to come. On November 4, the San Diego Chargers came to the Metrodome to

Chicago's Lance Briggs (number 55) can't stop Adrian during a run in the third quarter of the Bears-Vikings game, October 14, 2007. Adrian rushed for 224 yards in that game—including touchdown runs of 67, 73, and 35 yards.

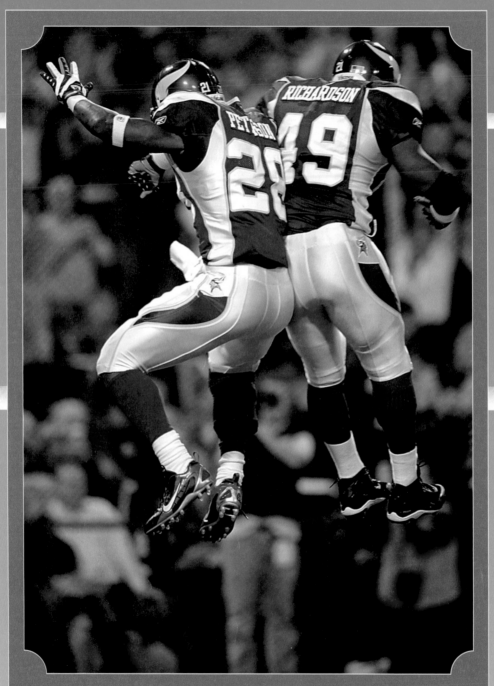

Adrian celebrates with teammate Tony Richardson (number 19) after scoring on a 16-yard run in a game against the Detroit Lions. The 42-10 victory evened the Vikings record at 6-6 and kept the team's playoff hopes alive.

take on the Vikings. Most people thought San Diego would win easily. The Chargers had four wins already, while the Vikings had won just twice. But Adrian had other ideas. He rushed for 296 yards and scored three more touchdowns as the Vikings upset San Diego 35–17.

The 296 yards Adrian gained against the Chargers was a personal best, of course. The total also broke the team record he had set just three weeks before. But Adrian's yardage that day was historic for another reason, too. No NFL player had ever rushed for that many yards in a game before. Halfway through his first professional season, Adrian had already put his name into the league's record books.

Struggles

Unfortunately Adrian's good fortune did not last. Just a week after the San Diego game, he struggled in a game against Green Bay. The Packers' defense held him to only 45 yards. Worse yet, he had to leave the game in the third quarter when he hurt his knee. The injury kept Adrian off the field for the next two games as well.

But Adrian returned with a bang on December 2, scoring two touchdowns and rushing for 116 yards as the Vikings defeated Detroit 42–10. Adrian had a terrible time in the team's next game, though. Although he carried the ball 14 times against the San Francisco 49ers, he was held to just 3 rushing yards—far below his average.

Adrian's struggles against San Francisco were not entirely his fault. The 49ers decided to try something new to keep the running back from dominating the game. They assigned more players than usual to guard against the run. That limited Adrian's ability to break through the defensive line. Each time he pushed past a San Francisco defender, it seemed that more 49ers were there to tackle him. But Adrian refused to use the 49ers' new defense as an excuse. As he said afterward,

❝I learned a lot from that game. . . . Just looking at the [video]tape, there's a lot of things I could have done different as far as footwork and little things like that . . . which would have changed the outcome on a couple plays.❞

Although Adrian had played poorly against San Francisco, the rest of the team had not. The Vikings beat the 49ers easily for their fourth victory in a row.

Disappointment

With just three games left in the 2007 regular season, the Vikings hoped to make the **playoffs**. Reaching the **postseason** was an important goal for Adrian. He had a personal goal, too: He wanted to set another NFL record. In 1983, Eric Dickerson of the Los Angeles (now St. Louis) Rams had rushed for 1,808 yards—the most ever for a first-year player. If he had three successful games, Adrian knew he might pass Eric's total.

On December 17, Adrian scored two touchdowns and ran for 78 yards as the Vikings beat the Bears for the second time in the season. But the Vikings lost to Washington the next week and ended the season with a heartbreaking **overtime** defeat in Denver. Minnesota's final record was eight wins and eight losses—not good enough to reach the playoffs. The last two games of the season were among Adrian's weakest of the year, too. He gained just 27 yards against Washington and 36 against Denver, and couldn't match Eric Dickerson's record.

Adrian was disappointed. At the same time, he had much to be proud of. He now held the single-game NFL rushing record. Only one player—San Diego running back LaDainian Tomlinson—had run for more than the 1,341 yards that Adrian gained during the season. Peterson was named to the NFC Pro Bowl roster. And he was an obvious choice for NFL **Rookie** of the Year, too. Adrian summed up his rookie season this way:

❝We accomplished some good things, but . . . we didn't accomplish our ultimate goal, and that was making it to the playoffs and giving ourselves a chance to go to the Super Bowl.❞

Family and Community

Like many star athletes, Adrian uses his talents to help others. While he is new to the Vikings and Minnesota, he began working with several community organizations in 2007. One of these was the Special Olympics, which helps mentally and physically handicapped people compete in sports. Another was the African American

CROSS-CURRENTS
For information about other Twin Cities sports stars who are fan favorites, read "More Minnesota Athletes." Go to page 54. ▶▶

After an outstanding first season in the NFL, Adrian was named the league's Rookie of the Year. Here, Adrian holds the award at a press conference before the Super Bowl.

Adoption Agency. This organization finds homes for black children who need them.

Adrian assists his hometown of Palestine, Texas, too. He plans to give money for a new football field at the local high school, for instance, and he hopes to set up a football camp for children. As he says,

"I definitely want to be known for the good things— giving back to the community, helping in the community, here [in Minnesota] as well as back at home. I want to be remembered for more than just what I do on the field. I think it's important to be known for the type of person I am, and the big heart I have."

In 2007, Adrian was among the league leaders in rushing yardage even though he missed two games due to injury. If the young running back stays healthy, he should accomplish great things in his career.

Adrian takes good care of his family, too. He bought his mother and stepfather a house, and he gave his father a BMW. He also let one of his brothers move in with him in Minnesota. Adrian's family also includes a young daughter, Adeja, born while he was still playing for the Oklahoma Sooners. Adeja lives with her mother in Texas, but she visits her father in Minnesota from time to time. People who know Adrian well say that money and fame have not spoiled him or made him snobbish.

Looking Ahead

It is always hard to predict a football player's future. The biggest reason is the possibility of getting hurt. Injuries are very common in football. Turning too quickly can damage a knee; being tackled can break a bone. Some of these injuries may keep a player on the bench for a few games. Others have a greater long-term impact. They may take away a player's speed, for example, or even end his career. Many experts worry that Adrian's hard, violent running style will quickly wear him down. One reporter predicts that Adrian will last no more than seven or eight seasons in the NFL.

But if Adrian can avoid injury, most people agree that he can have a great career. Strong and speedy, Adrian is determined to succeed. Even as a rookie he was already one of the best players in the NFL—and most players improve after their first season. That has to be a scary thought for Adrian's opponents! As journalist Michael Silver writes:

CROSS-CURRENTS

To learn about some NFL players whose careers were shortened by injuries, read "Danger on the Field." Go to page 55. ▶▶

> **❝[Adrian will] take on his next challenge the only way he knows—running headlong, fast and furious, [and] plowing through the pain.❞**

Conferences and Divisions

The 32 teams in the National Football League (NFL) are divided into two conferences: the National Conference (NFC) and the American Conference (AFC). Each conference has 16 teams. The conferences are also split into four divisions of four teams each. The NFC includes the NFC North, the NFC East, the NFC West, and the NFC South, and the AFC's four divisions are also called North, East, West, and South.

Playoffs

The divisions and conferences have two main purposes. One is to help determine which teams make the playoffs, sometimes called the postseason. Playoff games are held after the regular season ends. They match the best teams in each conference. Teams that lose are out of the competition. The playoffs end with the Super Bowl, which determines the league champion.

The four division winners in each conference automatically make the playoffs. In 2007, for instance, the Green Bay Packers won the NFC North, so they moved on to the postseason. Each conference also sends two other teams to the playoffs. These teams are known as wild cards. They are the teams that had the best records without winning their divisions. The NFC wild card teams in 2007 were Washington and the New York Giants.

In the first few games of the postseason, teams play other teams in their own conference. This system produces a champion for each conference. These two teams then meet in the Super Bowl. As a result, the Super Bowl is always between the AFC champion and the NFC champion. The 2007 season ended with the NFC champion New York Giants beating the New England Patriots, who won the AFC.

Schedule

The conferences and divisions are also used to plan schedules. Each year teams play two games against other teams in their own division. In the NFC North, for example, the Minnesota Vikings play two games each against Detroit, Chicago, and Green Bay. Teams also play six games against teams that are in their conference, but not in their division. In 2007 the Vikings played San Francisco, New York, Washington, and three other NFC teams.

Finally, teams play four games against teams in the other conference. The 2007 Vikings took on the teams of the AFC West—Denver, San Diego, Kansas City, and Oakland. In this way teams play most of their games against division rivals and other teams in their own conference. But they also get a chance to compare themselves to the clubs in the other conference.

(Go back to page 6.) ◀◀

All-Star Games and the Pro Bowl

The four major team sports in North America are football, baseball, hockey, and basketball. Each of these sports holds an all-star game every year. In an all-star game, the sport's top athletes play a game that doesn't count in the standings. Still, fans find the game fun to watch. And many players look forward to taking part in these games.

The Pro Bowl is the NFL's all-star game. In some important ways, though, it's different from the all-star games in other sports. Baseball, basketball, and hockey each schedule their all-star games for the middle of the season. In football, however, the Pro Bowl is held after the season is over. At the Pro Bowl, too, the NFL's usual rules are changed slightly to help players avoid injury. Other sports, though, stick with their regular rules.

Another difference involves where the game is played. Baseball, basketball, and hockey move their all-star games from city to city. The National Hockey League's all-star game, for example, was played in Atlanta, Georgia in 2008. The previous two games were held in Dallas, Texas, and St. Paul, Minnesota. Since 1980, in contrast, the NFL has held every Pro Bowl at Aloha Stadium in Honolulu, Hawaii. Differences like these make the Pro Bowl unique.

(Go back to page 7.) ◀◀

A ceremony is held on the field at Aloha Stadium in Honolulu before the 2008 Pro Bowl game. The NFL's annual all-star game is always held in Hawaii shortly after the Super Bowl.

Emmitt Smith

The Dallas Cowboys were a very strong team when Adrian was growing up. Part of the reason for their success was Emmitt Smith. Emmitt, who played in the NFL from 1990 to 2004, still holds the record for career rushing yards. He also won three Super Bowls and a Most Valuable Player award. Emmitt will almost certainly be elected to the professional Hall of Fame in 2010, when his name will be on the ballot for the first time.

To the Super Bowl

Emmitt Smith was born in Florida in 1969. He attended the University of Florida, where he became a star; he still holds many school records. In 1990, however, he decided to leave college early to turn pro. He was picked in the first round by the Cowboys that year.

The Cowboys had been a terrible team in 1989. They had won just one game all season. In 1990, Emmitt's first season as a pro, Dallas won seven games, a huge improvement over the year before. The next year, the Cowboys made the playoffs with a record of 11 wins and 5 losses. Although they didn't make it to the Super Bowl, they were now among the best teams in the NFL.

Then, in 1992, the Cowboys were even better.

During his 15-year career, Emmitt Smith was named to the Pro Bowl eight times. Emmitt set an NFL record for career rushing yardage, and his 175 touchdowns (164 rushing, 11 receiving) are second on the NFL's all-time list.

They won 13 regular season games, then won the NFC championship. Finally, they demolished the Buffalo Bills in the Super Bowl, 52–17. The following year, they won the Super Bowl again. Emmitt was a leader of these Cowboys teams, along with two other young players, quarter-back Troy Aikman and **wide receiver** Michael Irvin. Together they formed a powerful offensive unit that scored many points.

Playing Style

As a running back, Emmitt mostly ran with the ball, though he was sometimes asked to catch passes as well. Emmitt was admired for his ability to see the whole field as he played. It seemed that he could tell exactly where all the defenders were at any moment. That helped him decide which way to run without being tackled. He was also very fast, and he suffered few injuries during his playing career.

Emmitt may have been the best running back of his time, although some experts would argue that Barry Sanders of the Detroit Lions was better. In any case, he was an amazing player for many years. It's no surprise that Adrian Peterson, growing up in Texas, wanted to be just like him.

(Go back to page 12.) ◀◀

College Recruiting

Many colleges in the United States care deeply about their football programs. They want to have winning teams that can bring publicity and income to the college. As a result they try to find the best players they can.

Finding these players, though, takes time and money. College coaches spend hours learning about the best high school players. They watch these players in action, and they study accounts of their games. The schools also form a relationship with the players they want most. So coaches visit the players and talk about what their college programs have to offer.

Different programs offer different things. The strongest programs often play in bowl games—big and important games at the end of the college season. A successful school might remind a prospect that he will probably play in bowl games. Schools with weaker teams, in contrast, might promise an athlete that he will play a lot.

Many college programs also offer athletic scholarships to the best players. These scholarships pay most of a player's college expenses. That makes a scholarship a very big deal! In the end the top prospects consider all the offers they get from schools and choose the one they like best.

(Go back to page 15.) ◀◀

The Heisman Trophy

Several different organizations give awards to the best college football players each year. The most famous of these awards is called the Heisman Trophy. This award is named for John Heisman, who was a player and a coach in the late 1800s and early 1900s. Certain kinds of players are more likely to win the trophy than others. Over the years, for instance, most Heisman Trophy winners have played for good teams. Almost all of them are running backs or quarterbacks. And nearly all are college seniors.

The first Heisman Trophy was awarded in 1935. The winner was Jay Berwanger of the University of Chicago. The Philadelphia Eagles offered Berwanger a contract to play professionally, but Berwanger wasn't interested. At the time, professional football had relatively few fans compared to college football, and Berwanger chose to do other things instead.

More recently, however, nearly all Heisman Trophy winners have gone on to play for pro teams. Indeed, the list of Heisman winners includes a number of players who were extremely successful in the NFL. Some of these are Tony Dorsett of the University of Pittsburgh, Barry Sanders of Oklahoma State University, and Herschel Walker of the University of Georgia.

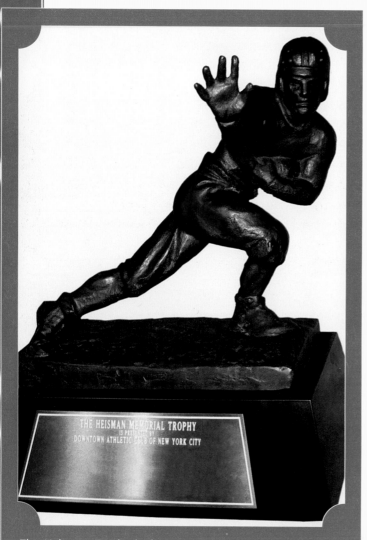

The Heisman Trophy is the most prestigious award a college football player can win. In 2004, Adrian became one of the few freshmen in college football history to be named a finalist for the award.

(Go back to page 17.) ◀◀

The 2007 Fiesta Bowl

The 2007 Fiesta Bowl matched Oklahoma against the Boise State Broncos. The Sooners came into the game with 11 wins and just 2 defeats. Boise State had won all 12 of its games. But the Broncos' opponents weren't as good as Oklahoma's. So, Boise State's record didn't seem as impressive. Most experts thought the Sooners would win easily.

The Broncos, however, scored first. At halftime they led 21–10. Early in the second half, they scored again to lead by 18 points. But the Sooners came back. Later in the third quarter, Adrian Peterson scored a touchdown. And an Oklahoma field goal in the fourth quarter narrowed Boise State's lead to 8. Still, the Sooners were running out of time.

An Amazing Finish

Now the action heated up. With less than two minutes left, Oklahoma scored a touchdown. Then they made a **two-point conversion**. Oklahoma had come back to tie the game at 28.

Boise State got the ball. But the Broncos didn't have it for long. The Sooners' Marcus Walker intercepted a pass—and returned it for a touchdown. Oklahoma led, 35–28. The Sooners had scored 25 points in a row. Now they were the ones who looked like winners.

Yet the game wasn't over. Boise State got the ball again. With only a few seconds left, the Broncos tried a trick play. The quarterback passed to one Bronco, who tossed the ball sideways to a teammate—who ran 35 yards for a touchdown. The game was tied again!

Overtime

The game now went to overtime. Each team had a chance to score. Oklahoma got the ball first. Adrian Peterson ran for a touchdown, and the Sooners kicked the extra point. They led 42–35. Now all they had to do was keep the Broncos from scoring.

The Broncos struggled to gain yards against the Sooner defense. Finally they had just one play left. If they didn't score, they would lose. Boise State used a trick again. They gave the ball to a running back, who surprised everyone by passing it into the end zone. Touchdown!

The Broncos could have kicked the extra point to tie the game once more and send it to another overtime. But their coach called for a two-point conversion instead. The Broncos used yet another trick play—and scored. Boise State had won one of the most exciting college football games ever played.

(Go back to page 25.) ◀◀

The Scouting Combine

The NFL scouting combine is officially known as the National Invitation Camp. It got its start in 1982. The first few camps were successful; teams learned a lot about players, and players had a chance to show the teams what they could do. The camps also saved time and money for players and teams alike. Before the combine, prospects might be evaluated seven or eight times by seven or eight different teams. Now, though, the teams join forces. Each player is evaluated just once, and the teams share the costs and the results.

Today more than 300 college players attend the scouting combine each year. They are chosen by a special committee made up of representatives from the NFL teams. The committee tries to predict which players will be picked in the next draft. Then committee members invite those players to take part in the combine.

The system isn't perfect. Some players are not invited to the scouting combine—but make the NFL anyway and go on to have fine careers. In contrast, some of the players invited to the combine never play in the pros at all. Still, after more than 25 years, the system works pretty well, and there are no plans to change it.

(Go back to page 28.) ◀◀

The Minnesota Vikings

The Minnesota Vikings represent the "Twin Cities" of Minneapolis and St. Paul. These two cities are the largest in Minnesota. They lie next to each other along the Mississippi River. Since 1981 the Vikings have played in the Metrodome, an indoor stadium in downtown Minneapolis.

A New Team

The Vikings entered the NFL in 1961. Like many new teams, they struggled at first. They won just three games in 1961 and two in 1962. In their first seven seasons, in fact, the Vikings never made it to the playoffs—and had only one winning record.

But in 1968 the Vikings' fortunes began to change. That year, Minnesota won its division for the first time. The following year, the Vikings won 12 regular season games and repeated as division champion. They even reached the Super Bowl—but lost to the Kansas City Chiefs 23–7.

More Success

From 1968 through 1980, the Vikings were among the NFL's top teams. Few teams in football history have been so good for so long. During these 13 years, the Vikings won 11 division titles and missed the playoffs just twice. They also played in three more Super Bowls. Unfortunately, they lost all three.

The Vikings had some great offensive players during these years. Quarterback Fran Tarkenton was the league's MVP in 1975, and running back Chuck Foreman was a big star, too. The Vikings were better known for their defense, however. They usually had one of the best in the league. In honor of the purple uniforms the Vikings wore, the defense was nicknamed the "Purple People Eaters."

Good Years and Bad

The early 1980s weren't good years for the Vikings. But the team soon bounced back. From 1987 to 2000, the Vikings once again made the postseason nearly every season. They weren't as dominant during these years as they had been during the 1970s, though. They were more often a wild card team than a division champion, and they never made it to the Super Bowl—not even in 1998, when they finished the regular season 15–1.

Minnesota's football team unveiled a new mascot, Viktor the Viking, before Adrian Peterson's first season. Since beginning play in the NFL in 1961, the Vikings have been one of the league's best teams, winning 16 division championships.

Since 2000 the Vikings haven't been a terrible team. But they haven't been an especially good one, either. Their fans are hoping that Adrian Peterson can help the Vikings be even more successful than they were in the 1970s—not just making the Super Bowl, but winning it!

(Go back to page 31.) ◀◀

More Minnesota Athletes

The Twin Cities of Minnesota are home to four major league sports teams. Besides the Vikings, there are also the Twins of Major League Baseball's American League; the Wild of the National Hockey League; and the Timberwolves, who play in the National Basketball Association. The Twins joined the American League in 1961, the same year that the Vikings entered the NFL. The other two teams are more recent. The Timberwolves entered the NBA in the 1989–90 season, and the Wild began NHL play in 2000–01.

Some Heroes

Sports fans in Minnesota have often had great players to cheer for. Hall of Famers Kirby Puckett, Rod Carew, and Harmon Killebrew all starred for the Twins. Cris Carter, Carl Eller, and Randy Moss each had fine seasons for the Vikings. Kevin Garnett was a brilliant basketball player in his time with the Timberwolves. Marian Gaborik holds many scoring records for the Wild.

Many of these players were not only good, though. They have also been admired by their fans. Twins fans loved Kirby Puckett for his joyful attitude toward baseball and life, for instance. Kevin Garnett was very popular as well. And Minnesota sports stars over the years have often done a great deal for their communities. Former Twins outfielder Torii Hunter is one example. Alan Page, who was a member of the Vikings' "Purple People Eater" defense, is another. Alan remained in Minnesota after his career was over. Today he serves as a judge on the state supreme court.

A New Role Model?

In recent years Minnesota sports fans suffered the loss of many of their favorite players. After the 2007 season, baseball star Torii Hunter left the Twins for the Los Angeles Angels, and his former teammate Johan Santana was traded to the New York Mets. Kevin Garnett moved on to the NBA's Boston Celtics. There were still a few big stars playing in Minnesota, and even a few with strong ties to the community. Twins catcher Joe Mauer, for instance, grew up in Minnesota and has impressed fans with his excellent play. And some of the Vikings have done plenty of work with charities in the Twin Cities.

But Minnesotans are ready for another role model from one of their sports teams—a great player with a good attitude and a desire to help others. Many journalists and fans in the area have wondered if Adrian Peterson might be the next great Minnesota athlete. Time will tell!

(Go back to page 42.) ◀◀

Danger on the Field

Football is a violent sport. The defense tries to tackle the man with the ball. The offense tries to knock down the defenders. Thus, injuries are common in the NFL. Over the years many fine players have had their careers interrupted or cut short by injuries.

One of these players was Bo Jackson. Bo was a marvelous athlete. He starred on the football team at Auburn University from 1982 to 1985, and he won the Heisman Trophy during his senior year. At the same time, he was a member of the school baseball team. Jackson chose to play both sports professionally. He did well, too. But in 1991 he injured his hip in a football playoff game with the Oakland Raiders. He never played professional football again. His baseball career ended soon after that, too.

Courtney Brown is another player whose career was damaged by injuries. The Cleveland Browns made him the first pick in the entire draft in 2000. Brown had a good first season with Cleveland. After that, however, he couldn't seem to stay healthy. He had problems with his ankles, biceps, feet, elbows, and knees. These injuries made his career shorter and less successful than it might have been.

(Go back to page 45.) ◀◀

Bo Jackson was a popular athlete who excelled at two professional sports—baseball and football—during the late 1980s and early 1990s. A hip injury during a 1991 football game ended his NFL career and shortened his baseball career.

1985 Adrian Peterson is born on March 21 in Palestine, Texas.

1998 Nelson Peterson, Adrian's father, is sent to prison for selling drugs.

2003 Adrian rushes for 2,960 yards in his final high school football season.

2004 Adrian graduates from Palestine High School.

He runs for 1,925 yards as a freshman at the University of Oklahoma, setting a new record for first-year college players.

He is named a First Team All-American by the Associated Press.

He finishes second in the balloting for the Heisman Trophy.

2005 Adrian rushes for 1,108 yards and 14 touchdowns, including an 84-yard TD run.

He is named to the All-Big 12 Conference Team.

2006 Nelson Peterson is released from prison in October.

Adrian misses several games due to injury, but ends the season with more than 1,000 yards rushing.

2007 Adrian's stepbrother, Chris Parish, is murdered in February, just before Adrian takes part in the annual NFL scouting combine.

On April 28, the Minnesota Vikings pick Adrian seventh in the NFL draft.

In a November 4 game against San Diego, Adrian runs for 296 yards, setting a new NFL record.

2008 Adrian is chosen as the Most Valuable Player of the Pro Bowl, played on February 10.

College Statistics

Year	Team	Rushing Attempts	Rushing Yards	Rushing TDs	Receptions	Receiving Yards	Receiving TDs
2004	Oklahoma	339	1,925	15	5	12	0
2005	Oklahoma	220	1,108	14	9	50	0
2006	Oklahoma	188	1,012	12	10	135	1

Pro Statistics

Year	Team	Rushing Attempts	Rushing Yards	Rushing TDs	Receptions	Receiving Yards	Receiving TDs
2007	Minnesota	238	1,341	12	19	268	1

Awards

2003 Hall Trophy as best high school player in the United States

2004 Runner-up in Heisman Trophy voting

2004 AP All-America First Team

2007 NFL Rookie of the Year and Offensive Rookie of the Year

2008 Pro Bowl MVP

Books and Periodicals

Athlon Sports. *Sooner Pride: Oklahoma Spirit Shines Through an Unforgettable Season*. Chicago: Triumph Books, 2005.

Craig, Mark. "New Viking Carries Heartache." Minneapolis *Star Tribune*, (April 30, 2007).

Hack, Damon. "The Virtue of Patience." *Sports Illustrated*, (October 15, 2007).

Krawczynski, John. "Peterson's Parents Lay Groundwork for Success." *USA Today*, (April 29, 2007).

Silver, Michael. "Full Speed Ahead." *Sports Illustrated*, (April 30, 2007)..

Stallard, Mark, ed. *Echoes of Oklahoma Football*. Chicago: Triumph Books, 2007.

Zulgad, Judd. "Getting to Know You." Minneapolis *Star Tribune*, (February 20, 2008).

Web Sites

http://cbs.sportsline.com/nfl

This site includes articles, results, statistics, and links to other information about the NFL.

http://www.vikings.com

The official site of the Minnesota Vikings gives team schedules, results of games, and information on players.

http://www.nfl.com/

The NFL's official site includes statistics, articles, videos, and other content that relates to the NFL and its players.

http://sportsillustrated.cnn.com/football/nfl/

The *Sports Illustrated* magazine's Web site, which provides news, scores, and other information about pro football.

http://www.soonersports.com/sports/m-footbl/okla-m-footbl-body.html

Oklahoma University's athletics Web site includes this page about the college's football program. The site provides many links, some videos, and historical information about the football team.

http://sports.yahoo.com/ncaaf/players/117290;_ylt=AkODz_XDVXhdL PkjNYhEIwvA.88F

This Web page gives biographical information about Adrian Peterson and statistical information about his three seasons of college football, broken down by game.

The Web sites mentioned in this book were active at the time of publication. The publisher is not responsible for Web sites that have changed their addresses or discontinued operation since the date of publication. The publisher will review and update the Web site addresses each time the book is reprinted.

bowl game—a special game played by two college teams after the end of the season. There are more than 30 bowl games today.

conference—a group of teams that play most of their games against one another. The NFL has the American Conference and the National Conference; there are many college conferences.

draft—the NFL's method of assigning college players to pro teams, held each spring. During this process, NFL teams take turns picking, or drafting, players.

end zone—the strip of the playing field beyond the goal line. A player who catches a pass in the opponents' end zone or carries the ball into the end zone has scored a touchdown.

extra point—a play worth one point, used only after a touchdown. A team that scores a touchdown can choose to have a player try to kick the ball between the goalposts. If the player is successful, the extra point is added to the team's score.

kickoff—the opening play to begin a game or after a scoring play, in which one team kicks the ball to the other.

MVP (Most Valuable Player)—award given to the player who has done the most to help his team in a game or during the season.

overtime—extra time added to a game that is tied after the second half is ended.

playoffs—a series of games held after the regular NFL season is over. The playoffs are limited to the best teams and end with the Super Bowl championship game.

postseason games—playoff games; games that are played after the regular season is over.

preseason games—games played by NFL teams before the regular season begins. These games do not count in the standings.

Pro Bowl—a game played after the NFL season ends by the best players in the league. The game does not count in the standings.

quarterback—the football player who leads the offense. He may pass the ball or run with it.

regular season games—games that count in the standings. NFL teams play 16 regular season games, college teams play fewer than that.

rookie—a player in his first year as a professional.

running back—a football player whose main job is to run with the ball.

rushing—football term used to describe running with the ball.

scout—a person who watches and evaluates players. Scouts for NFL teams may study college players to determine which players to choose in the draft, or they may watch upcoming NFL opponents of their team to decide how to play against them.

scouting combine—an event held each winter in which NFL teams watch and talk to some of the nation's top college football players.

training camp—an event held by each NFL team during the summer, designed to get players ready for the upcoming season.

two-point conversion—a play worth two points, used only after a touchdown. A team that scores a touchdown can try to run or pass the ball into the end zone from a short distance away. If a player can reach the end zone with the ball, the team is awarded two extra points.

wide receiver—a football player whose main job is to catch passes.

page 7 "I'm dedicated to being. . . " John Clayton, "It Took All Day for the NFC to Win the Pro Bowl" ESPN.com (February 10, 2008), http://sports.espn.go.com/nfl/columns/story?columnist=clayton_john&id=3240240.

page 9 "Can I top this. . . " "Mission Accomplished: Peterson Claims MVP" *Houston Chronicle* (February 11, 2008), p. 3.

page 10 "I ran around . . . " Elizabeth Newman, "First Person: Adrian Peterson" SI.com(February 20, 2007), http://sportsillustrated.cnn.com/2007/players/02/20/first.person0226/.

page 12 "It was a hard time . . . " John Krawczynski, "Peterson's Parents Lay Groundwork for Success" *USA Today* (April 29, 2007), http://www.usatoday.com/sports/football/2007-04-29-2583963380_x.htm.

page 15 "Adrian's a pretty unique kid . . ." Mark Craig, "New Viking Carries Heartache" Minneapolis *Star Tribune* (April 30, 2007), p 1A.

page 22 "Even though he was away . . . " Newman, "First Person."

page 22 "[Adrian is] a guy . . . " Mike Max, "Adrian Peterson Credits Family for Success" WCCO.com (May 21, 2007), http://wcco.com/sports/Adrian.Peterson.Minnesota.2.371969.html.

page 25 "That describes everything to me . . . " Michael Silver, "Full Speed Ahead" SI.com (April 30, 2007), http://vault.sportsillustrated.cnn.com/vault/article/magazine/MAG1110911/2/index.htm.

page 30 "You're gonna show 'em! . . . " Silver, "Full Speed Ahead."

page 30 "Peterson's arguably the biggest playmaker . . . " Peter Schrager, "Mock Draft 9.0" Foxsports.com http://msn.foxsports.com/nfl/story/6670816/Mock-draft-9.0:-Peterson-may-be-steal-of-draft.

page 32 "He was . . . big, bright-eyed . . . " Judd Zulgad, "Getting to Know You" Minneapolis *Star Tribune* (February 20, 2008), p. C1.

page 33 "Whatever the team [needs] . . . " Scott Wright, "Vikings enter A.D. era" *The Daily Oklahoman* (April 29, 2007), p. 1.

page 35 "[H]e's a very intelligent . . . " Kevin Seifert, "Top Pick Peterson Signs Deal" Washington: Knight Ridder Tribune Business News (July 30, 2007), p. 1.

page 38 "He can run . . . " Damon Hack, "The Virtue of Patience" *Sports Illustrated* (October 15, 2007), p. 34+.

page 41 "I learned a lot . . . " Don Seeholzer, "Minnesota Vikings' Adrian Peterson Learns from 49ers Game" McClatchy-Tribune Business News (December 15, 2007).

page 42 "We accomplished some good things . . . " Judd Zulgad, "AD Offers No Excuse for Feeble Finish" Minneapolis *Star Tribune* (December 31, 2007), p. C9.

page 44 "I definitely want . . . " Jim Souhan, "Peterson in Line to Fill a Major Void" Washington: McClatchy Tribune Business News (December 2, 2007).

page 45 "[Adrian will] take on . . . " Silver, "Full Speed Ahead."

Numbers in ***bold italics*** refer to captions.

NORTHEASTERN
MIDDLE SCHOOL LIBRARY

Stephen Currie is a writer and teacher who has published dozens of books for children and young adults. His nonfiction book *Thar She Blows* was chosen a Best Book for the Teen Age by the New York Public Library, and he has appeared in a History Channel documentary about women inventors. He has written extensively about sports, including many articles about baseball and a short biography of soccer star Mia Hamm. He lives in New York State and enjoys kayaking, snowshoeing, and bicycling.

PICTURE CREDITS

page

5: IOS Photos

6: James E. Foehl/U.S.DoD/NMI

8: Kirk Aeder/Icon SMI

11: KRT Photos

13: IOS Photos

14: BenA1974/SPCS

17: absolutwade/SPCS

18: Sports Illustrated/NMI

20: Zuma Press

23: IOS Photos

24: Billy Adams/Icon SMI

27: Nick Laham/Getty Images

29: Kevin Terrell/NFL/SPCS

31: Chris McGrath/Getty Images

32: S.Levy/SPCS

34: Tom Dahlin/WireImage

37: Tom Dahlin/Getty Images

39: Chicago Tribune/MCT

40: Minneapolis Star Tribune/MCT

43: UPI Photo

44: Minnesota Vikings/PRMS

47: ZE/SPCS

48: University of Florida/SPCS

50: Sotheby's/PRMS

53: Minnesota Vikings/PRMS

55: MLB Photos/SPCS

Front cover: Stephen Dunn/Getty Images

Front cover inset: Minnesota Vikings/PRMS